THE HOWLAND HOMESTEAD

THE HOWLAND HOMESTEAD

BY
Pilgrim John Howland

KALPAZ

ISBN: 978-93-5128-692-9(PB)

First Published in 1911
Indian Reprint in 2017

Published by

Kalpaz Publications
C-30, Satyawati Nagar,
Delhi – 110052
E-mail: kalpaz@hotmail.com
Website: kalpazpublications.com
Ph.: +91-9212142040

Society of the Descendants of Pilgrim John Howland of the Ship "Mayflower"

The annual meeting of the Society of the Descendants of Pilgrim John Howland of the Ship "Mayflower" is called for Saturday, September 2, 1911. at 2 P. M., at the Samoset House, Plymouth, Mass. Train leaves South Station, Boston, at 8.42 A. M., reaching Plymouth at 10.40. Fare 75c. Or by Boat, leaving Rowe's Wharf at 10 A. M., arriving in Plymouth at 1 P. M.

On arrival of the train at Plymouth members will be met by the Secretary and a visit paid to the grave of John Howland, to the church to see the Memorial Pulpit given by Descendants of John Howland, and to the old Howland House on Carver Street, for the purchase of which a considerable sum has already been subscribed.

Dinner will be served at the Samoset House at 1 P. M. Dinner tickets $1.00 each. Please notify the Samoset House by August 30 if you intend to be present in order that seats may be reserved for you. It is expected that Capt. J. Henry Sears, President Cape Cod Pilgrim Memorial Association, will be a guest at the dinner. Business meeting at 2 P. M. Returning, trains leave Plymouth at 3.55 and 5.55 P. M., arriving in Boston at 5.17 and 7.17 P. M.

You are cordially invited to attend this meeting of the Society, which seeks to unite all descendants of the "Beloved Pilgrim" in all parts of our land. Please extend this invitation to any descendants of John Howland whom you may know.

"The Howland Homestead" the new magazine issued by the Society is just out. Published quarterly. Interesting to all Howland descendants. July number contains ancestry of John Howland in England, The Howland Arms, also account of the work being done for the preservation of the old Howland House at Plymouth. Price $1.00 a year. Single copies 25 cents. Subscribe now and mail a copy to your friends. The Personal and Genealogical Column will be a feature. Letters of inquiry should contain a self-addressed stamped envelope for reply. Subscriptions should be sent to

MRS. NELSON V. TITUS, Secretary and Treasurer
Squantum P. O., Quincy, Mass.

Aug. 1, 1911.

The Howland Homestead.

VOL. I. BOSTON, MASS., JULY, 1911. No. 1.

"One small candle may light a thousand."

WE present herewith to the Descendants of Pilgrim John Howland the first number of the magazine "The Howland Homestead," hoping that it will supply a long-felt want and give accurate information of the work of the Society, to tell what has been accomplished in the past and what we hope to accomplish in the future. To no other Society in the world has been given such an honor or such a privilege — to preserve and hand down to posterity the last house left standing to-day in Plymouth where the feet of the Mayflower Pilgrims have trod, whose walls, if they could speak, would tell us how John Howland and his wife looked when they passed about the rooms — some apparently in the same condition to-day as they were 244 years ago.

The Editor of this magazine asks your help in furthering the plans of the Society. Many Howlands are scattered about all over the world. To such, a visit to Plymouth would be the event of a lifetime, but if they cannot come to Plymouth, this little magazine hopes to bring Plymouth to them and make them feel that although far away, they are bound by ties of kindred to those who are working here to save the venerable house which will grow more interesting as years pass on.

The photograph shows that to the left of the house, in fact only twenty feet from it, is a livery stable, which stands on part of the original Howland lot. It greatly increases the danger of fire and should be removed. The owner offers to sell it to the Society for a reasonable sum. If the stable could be torn down, and a beautiful lawn graded and set with old-fashioned shrubs and flowers, it would add greatly to the Homestead. Will not some of our Howland Descendants start a fund for the removal of the stable and for the necessary work? About $5,000 will be needed. As soon as the deed of the house is in the possession of the Society, the next work must be to restore the house to the style of the Colonial days and remove the stable. We ask your help — subscribe for the magazine, and mail a copy to any Howland Descendants you may know. Letters of inquiry should contain a self-addressed envelope for reply.

Address all communications to

MRS. NELSON V. TITUS, *Treasurer*,
Squantum P. O., Quincy, Mass.

SOCIETY OF THE DESCENDANTS OF PILGRIM JOHN HOWLAND OF THE SHIP "MAYFLOWER."

OFFICERS.

President, Mr. CLARENCE STUART WARD, Boston.
Vice-President, Rear Admiral GEORGE C. REMEY, U. S. N., Washington, D. C.
Secretary and Treasurer, Mrs. NELSON V. TITUS, Squantum, Quincy, Mass.

This Society was organized at Plymouth, Mass., May 18, 1897, for the following purposes:—

> "To perpetuate the memory of our ancestors, John Howland and his wife, Elizabeth Tilley, who, braving the perils of the deep, were among that little band of Pilgrims who landed from the Ship 'Mayflower' on Plymouth Rock, Dec. 21, 1620; to preserve and publish any manuscript relating to the families of John Howland and his wife, to erect and keep in good repair a memorial to their memory in the Pilgrim Church at Plymouth, to assist in prosecuting research in England and Holland to discover their ancestry; to preserve and if possible acquire possession of the Howland House in Plymouth, and to endeavor to acquire a better knowledge of the causes which led them to emigrate to the new world."

The Memorial Pulpit to our ancestors has been placed in the Pilgrim Church at Plymouth, and a silver tablet upon it states that it is the gift of the descendants of John Howland.

The work now undertaken is the acquisition and preservation by the Society of the Howland House in Plymouth, built in 1667.

As many descendants of John Howland live in distant parts of the country and cannot attend meetings, the entrance fee to the Society has been placed at $1.00 with annual dues of but $1.00 a year, to cover postage and printing. Life membership $20.00.

If the old house is secured by this Society it is probable that the annual meeting of the Society will be held there each summer.

You are cordially invited to join the Society, which seeks to unite all descendants of the "Beloved Pilgrim" in all parts of our land. Please extend this invitation to any descendants of John Howland whom you may know. Application blanks will be furnished, and any further information will be given by addressing the Secretary.

"Fresh seeds for all the time to be
Are in my hand to sow,
Whereby for others, and for me
Undreamed of fruit may grow."

AN APPEAL FOR THE PRESERVATION OF THE HOWLAND HOUSE IN PLYMOUTH, MASS.

The famous old Howland House on Sandwich Street, Plymouth, built in 1667, is of historic interest as one of the oldest houses in America, it having withstood the ravages of time for 244 years. Unless it is purchased it may be torn down, as have been other old Plymouth houses, when it is no longer rentable. It is now being used as a tenement. A grave mistake has been made in the past in allowing these famous old Pilgrim dwellings to be destroyed. No house now standing in Plymouth is more nearly associated with the Pilgrims than this one.

Mr. William T. Davis, the historian, in his "Ancient Land-marks of Plymouth" says of the Howland House "Owned and occupied as it undoubtedly was by Jabez Howland before the death of his father and mother, it is fair to presume that its floors have been trodden by these two passengers of the 'Mayflower' and its walls have listened to their voices. Let this ancient structure be added to the list of Pilgrim memorials and share with the Rock our veneration and respect."

Our ancestor, John Howland, was called by his Pilgrim Associates the "Beloved Pilgrim."

The record of John Howland's death says: "He was a godly man and an ancient professor in the ways of Christ. He lived until he attained above 80 years in the world. He was one of the first comers into this land and proved a usefull instrument of good in his place, and was the last one that was left of those that came over in the ship called the 'Mayflower' that lived in Plymouth."

This appeal to save this venerable house, which should be sacred to all the descendants of John Howland and his wife, Elizabeth Tilley Howland, is made in confidence that a cordial and prompt response will save this dwelling. The owner, who has no family interest in it, offers to sell it to the Society for $2,000, which is considered a very reasonable sum.

We wish to restore and furnish the house in the style of the olden days, to open the old fire-place, hang a crane in the chimney and light a fire once more upon the long silent hearth and then place some suitable person in the house as care-taker to show the house to members of the Society and visitors. Here once a year the scattered Howland Descendants may meet and recall the scenes of long ago.

To do this, $5,000 is needed; of this sum $2,000 to be paid for the property, $1,000 to be spent for repairs, and $2,000 to be placed in a fund, the income from which will assure the preservation forever of this historic dwelling. About $1,100 has already been subscribed.

In order to secure the property at this price and carry out the proposed plans it is necessary to raise this amount by October 1st. Will you help us.

All descendants of John Howland are earnestly asked to try to interest other descendants in this patriotic work. Checks should be made payable to the "Howland House Fund" and sent to the Treasurer. Subscriptions will be acknowledged and any further information will be given by addressing

MRS. NELSON V. TITUS,

Secretary and Treasurer.

Society of the Descendants of Pilgrim John Howland
of the Ship "Mayflower."

P. O. Address, Squantum, Quincy, Mass.

"In passing the old milestones I feel like taking off my hat, in honor of the first settlers who placed them there."

G. Augustus Hinckley, Barnstable.

[A Descendant of John Howland. Born Aug. 15, 1822 : Died Aug 7, 1909.]

ANNUAL MEETING, AUGUST 4, 1910.

The John Howland Descendants met at the ancestral house in Plymouth, August 4, 1910, and incorporated the Society of the Descendants of Pilgrim John Howland of the Ship Mayflower, and took steps to preserve the old homestead at Plymouth. Dinner was served at the Samoset House, and all present signed the articles of incorporation. After the banquet at the Samoset House, the Society visited the old house and also the grave of John Howland, where a laurel wreath was placed. Many of them remained over night at Plymouth, going on the next day to the celebration at Provincetown, of the dedication of the Pilgrim Monument.

Among those present were, Rear Admiral and Mrs. George C. Remey, U. S. N., of Washington, D. C., Mrs. M. J. Perkins of New York, Mr. and Mrs. Summerfield Hagerty and Miss Stran of New York, Mrs. Arthur Young, Miss Mildred Young, and Miss Caroline Young, of Winthrop, Mass., Mrs. Edwin L. Burnham of Portland, Maine, Mrs. G. W. Smith of Fairfield, Conn., Mr. and Mrs. Lansing of Swampscott, Mr. Clarence S. Ward of Brookline, Miss H. B. Pierce and Mrs. N. V. Titus of Quincy, Mass., Mr. and Mrs. C. H. Armstrong, Bridgeport, Conn., S. F. Howland, New York.

The fine steamboat "Betty Alden," which leaves Rowe's Wharf, Boston, daily for Plymouth, gives a delightful sail. Passengers can spend several hours at Plymouth and returning, reach Boston at 6.15 P. M.

"Next to the fugitives whom Moses led out of Egypt, the little shipload of outcasts who landed at Plymouth are destined to influence the future of the world."—*James Russell Lowell.*

THE HOWLAND ARMS.

The heraldic description of the Howland arms is as follows: — Argent, two bars sable; in chief three lions rampant of the second. Crest: A lion passant sable, ducally gorged or. In ordinary English, this means that the field of the shield is white (*argent*) with two horizontal bars of black (*sable*); the lions and the crest are also black. Sometimes the crest used is a leopard with a coronet of gold (*or*) about his throat, as in the engraving.

THE ANCESTRY OF JOHN HOWLAND OF THE "MAYFLOWER."

For many years the descendants of John Howland, in America, had sought in vain to discover his ancestry in England. In 1879, several of his descendants subscribed a sum of money to make a thorough research among the records in England and employed for this purpose Col. Joseph L. Chester, a barrister and noted antiquarian in London, England. The result of his investigations, as reported by Mr. L. M. Howland, was as follows:

"Col. Chester's investigations show that the surname Howland is found in no other county in England than Essex and originally in no other locality in that county except Newport, Wicken and their immediate vicinity.

"At the time of the birth of John Howland, the Pilgrim, it appears that there were several distinct families by the name of Howland in England who were all in some way connected. The head of the line was JOHN HOWLAND, of Newport Pond, in the county of Essex, whose will was proved April 12, 1550.

"His son, JOHN HOWLAND, the citizen and salter, was born in Newport Pond, and married Agnes, daughter of John Greenaway of Winton Co., Norfolk. His brother, Ralph Howland, became distinguished as an Alderman of London and master of the Grocers Company. John[2] Howland, the citizen and salter, had eleven sons and one daughter, who died an infant.

"Several of his sons attained eminence, the most notable of whom were: the eldest son, The Right Reverend Richard[3] Howland, Bishop of Peterborough, whose painting is extant and has been photographed.

"John[3] of London, the second son, was baptized Aug. 10, 1541, and buried in the Church of St. Mary's, Middlesex. He married Emme, daughter of Nicholas Revell, citizen and grocer of London. His son John[4] Howland, is the one who has always hitherto been supposed to be identical with John Howland of the "Mayflower," but Mr. Chester proves that the former died unmarried and was buried in England.

"The seventh son, Sir Giles Howland, bought large estates in Surrey, but left no male issue.

"The second family of Howland in England is traced back to John[1] Howland 'of the Stone,' of Wicken Co., Essex, living in 1496, who died about 1509. Of his son, John[2] Howland, nothing is known but that he named his youngest child John Howland. This John[3] was married at Newport to Blanche, daughter of William Nightingale, gentleman. The youngest child, Jeffrey[4] Howland, was baptized at Newport, 29 July, 1593. He became a citizen and grocer of London and afterwards succeeded to the Streatham estates of Sir Giles Howland, of the family previously mentioned, to whom he was closely related, as not only this fact proves, but also the constant mention of him as 'cousin,' in the wills of the other line.

"The family of Jeffrey[4] Howland ending in an heiress, these vast estates passed into the hands of the Duke of Bedford by the marriage of Wrotherley, 2nd Duke, to Elizabeth, "only daughter and heir.' The property was so considerable that the title of Baron Howland was conferred upon him by the Crown.

"There was then a third contemporaneous John Howland, called 'of the Wood, in Wicken,' evidently to distinguish him from the others, but of him the London records reveal nothing.

"A fourth John Howland, distinguished as a 'Husbandman,' having children baptized in Newport from 1576 to 1588, is also to be mentioned as being of a separate family. His history and that of his children can be found by reference to the Newport registers.

"A certain Robert Howland, buried in Debden, Essex, 23 Nov., 1616, had a son named John, who was living at Newport in 1616.

"Just at the close of the investigations of Col. Chester, when the funds with which he had been furnished were exhausted, he found another family of Howlands, consisting of the following sons, Humphrey, citizen and draper of London, whose will was proved July 10, 1646; George, of St. Dunstan's in the East, London; also Arthur, John, and Henry. These last three brothers in the order named, were to receive by Humphrey's will, dated May 28, 1646, £8, £4, £4, out of the debt due the testator Humphrey by Mr. Ruck of New England.

"There is some proof that these brothers, Arthur, John and Henry, whose names appear in the records of Plymouth Colony, were the American ancestors of the Howland family, and perhaps the strongest evidence is found in the fact that John Ruck was living in Salem, Mass., at this time.

"Savage refers to him as 'John Ruck' of Salem, son of Thomas, born in England, about 1627. He was made Freeman of Massachusetts, Plymouth Colony, in 1640, kept a tavern in Salem in 1663, was selectman of Salem in 1686, and represented it in the General Court in 1685–9. In Felt's

Annals of Salem is this paragraph: '1659—A grist mill is allowed on South River above Mr. Ruck's house.'

"It is plain that Mr. John Ruck owed £16 to Humphrey Howland, who willed it to his brothers then in Plymouth. George Howland's estate was administered upon by Annie Howland, widow of his brother Humphrey, July 11, 1646. She was also executrix of the estate of her husband. She was buried at Barking, County of Essex, Dec. 20, 1653. Her will was dated 10 Dec., 1653, proved 22 Nov., 1654, by William Courtoyse, to whom she left considerable legacies. Doubtless these Howland lads were of the pilgrim band who had their headquarters for a while at Scrooby in England, and, in the spring of 1608, went to Amsterdam, where they resided a year, when most of them removed to Leyden, 22 miles distant. Here they remained until they emigrated to New England. Their social life in England is unknown, but it is fair to presume that the pilgrim community at Leyden was made up of members representing all the different classes of English life, bound together by a common religious faith, regardless of those differences in education, culture and social standing which were insignificant in their eyes compared with their real bond of union." It was this disregard of social conditions which doubtless planted in their hearts the democratic seed, which later took root and grew in the soil of New England.

"John Howland of the 'Mayflower' held to the original faith of the Puritans during his life and was a consistent member of the Orthodox Church till his death. Arthur and Henry were Quakers. Many of their descendants for many generations, and some are yet, members of the Friends Society. On the other hand, no descendant of John (1) has been found who was of that sect."

John Howland, the thirteenth signer of the Mayflower compact, came in the 'Mayflower.' At that time, he was 28 years of age, and according to Prince, was a member of Governor Carver's family. It is probable that Carver, seeing elements in Howland's character that made him confident that he would become a valuable addition to the Pilgrim Colony, advanced him the money needed for the passage to the New World. He thus became attached to the family of Governor Carver. Bradford speaks of him as a 'man-servant,' but it is probable that the word was used much as we speak of an employé to-day. Attention is called to the fact that John Howland signed the Compact in the cabin of the 'Mayflower' before such men as Hopkins, the Tilleys, Cooke, Rogers and Priest, which does not indicate that he was merely a servant. In any event, he soon proved to be one of the most energetic and valuable members of the Colony, and whenever there was any dangerous work to be done or expedition sent out, John Howland's name will be found among the party.

He was one of the ten 'principal men' who with eight seamen were 'sente out' on the 6th Dec. following the landing, to discover a location suitable for their future home. In 1627, he was associated with Governor Bradford and six other principal men in the Colony in a contract made with the London Merchant Adventurers, in which they agreed to give them £1800 for the relinquishment of their claims upon the Plymouth lands, and also to assume the Colony debts amounting to £2400 more. As a consideration for this, the 'undertakers,' as they were called, were to have the monopoly of the whole trade of the Colony for six years. In 1633, John Howland was elected an Assistant in the government of the Colony, which office he held for several years.

He had the chief management of the trading post on the Kennebec where his firmness was tested by the headstrong and reckless Hocking, and for 18 years he was representative of the Town of Plymouth to the General Court of the Colony. The frequency with which his name occurs in the Plymouth Records furnishes abundant evidence that he was one of the most energetic and efficient members of the Plymouth Colony.

THE annual meeting of the Society of the Descendants of Pilgrim John Howland of the ship "Mayflower" is called for Saturday, September 2, 1911, at 2 P. M., at the Samoset House, Plymouth, Mass. Train leaves South Station, Boston, at 8.42 A. M., reaching Plymouth at 10.40. Fare, 75c. Or by boat, leaving Rowe's Wharf at 10 A. M., arriving in Plymouth at 1 P. M.

On arrival of the train at Plymouth, members will be met by the Secretary and a visit paid to the grave of John Howland; to the church to see the Memorial Pulpit given by Descendants of John Howland, and to the old Howland House on Sandwich Street, for the purchase of which a considerable sum has already been subscribed.

Dinner will be served at the Samoset House at 1 P. M. Dinner tickets, $1.00 each. Please notify the Samoset House by August 30, if you intend to be present, in order that seats may be reserved for you. It is expected that Capt. J. Henry Sears, President Cape Cod Pilgrim Memorial Association, will be a guest at the dinner. Business meeting at 2 P. M. Returning, trains leave Plymouth at 3.55 and 5.55 P. M., arriving in Boston at 5.17 and 7.17 P. M.

You are cordially invited to attend this meeting of the Society, which seeks to unite all descendants of the "Beloved Pilgrim" in all parts of our land. Please extend this invitation to any descendants of John Howland whom you may know.

L. B. TITUS, *Sec'y and Treas.*

THE OLD HOWLAND HOUSE.

The old Howland house was formerly known as the Carver house on Sandwich Street, and was originally a six or eight post house, but the old rafters indicate that the roof has been raised three times. It was erected by Jacob Mitchell, probably between 1665 and 1670, as he married in 1666 and bought the lot in 1667. He sold it to Jabez Howland undoubtedly before John Howland's death. The main room of the old house remains in nearly its original condition, and if its walls could speak, they would repeat the words of John and his wife Elizabeth.

Jabez Howland, when he removed to Bristol, R. I., in 1680, sold the house to Elkanah Watson; then it was sold by John Watson, son of the above, to Stephen Churchill. Mr. Churchill sold a portion of it to Ephraim Little in 1716, and it was sold in 1775 to Benjamin Churchill, and in 1784 it was sold to Joseph Thomas and Ephraim Spooner. In 1790 Joseph Thomas sold the house to Nathaniel Carver. It remained in the Carver family until 1867, when it was sold to Joseph E. Sherman and by him to Barnabas H. Holmes, who, a few years ago, conveyed it to his daughter, Miss Helen R. Holmes, of Washington, D. C., who has owned it to the present time, when arrangements have been made by the Society to purchase it.

In 1627, John Howland's family consisted of himself, his wife Elizabeth, his son John and daughter Desire, who was named after Desire Minter, the faithful friend of Elizabeth Tilley. Elizabeth Tilley was fourteen years old at the time of her parents' death in 1621, soon after their arrival in New England. She married John Howland about 1624. Elizabeth Howland was a woman of superior natural ability and earnest Christian faith, and a helpmeet indeed to the sturdy Pilgrim. She passed the closing days of her life with her daughter Lydia Brown at Swansea, where she died, according to the Swansea town records, "21-12-1687, aged 80 years," which prove she was but thirteen years of age when she arrived at Plymouth.

In the next issue of the magazine will be given the text of John Howland's will and also that of his wife Elizabeth, and a brief account of Jabez Howland, who owned the old Howland house.

A full account of the Annual meeting of the Society of the Descendants of Pilgrim John Howland of the "Ship Mayflower," to be held at Plymouth, Sept. 2, 1911, will be published in the October "Homestead."

In our next issue we shall publish a list of all contributors to the Howland House Fund. Shall we find your name there? If a receipt for money sent is desired, the Treasurer will greatly appreciate it if a self-addressed stamped envelope accompanies the same.

The furnishing of three rooms in the old house at Plymouth has been promised by the following persons, who will in this way honor their ancestors. Mr. John Crocker Foote of Belvidere, Illinois, will furnish the living room in memory of his mother, Mrs. Mary Crocker Foote ; Mrs. Summerfield Hagerty will furnish another room in memory of her grandmother, Mrs. Dorcas Gardner Swift, a descendant of John Howland in the Gardner line. Mrs. Lucy E. Wallace, and her cousin, Mrs. Lillie B. Titus, will furnish another room in memory of their grandfather, Captain James Huckins, a descendant through Thomas Huckins of Barnstable from Hope Howland, a daughter of John Howland of the "Mayflower."

Miss Mary E. Knowles, Providence, R. I., has donated some interesting articles for the kitchen, including old candle-moulds, leathern bellows, and other articles of the Colonial period. Mrs. Ella H. Stratton of Hopkinton. Mass., has offered to make the old-fashioned corn-husk mats to furnish the porches of the house when restored.

Bradford says of John Howland : "And as they lay at hull, in a mighty storme, a lustie younge man, called John Howland, coming upon some occasion above ye gratings, was, with a seele of ye ship, throwne into ye sea, but it pleased God yt he cought hould of ye top saile halliards, which hunge overboard & ran out at length : he held his hould (though he was sundrie fadomes underwater) till he was hald up by ye same rope to ye brime of ye waters, and then with a boat hooke and other means got into ye ship againe & his life was saved. And though he was somewhat ill with it, yet he lived many years after and became a profitable member, both in ye church and in ye comon welthe."

Visitors to Plymouth are advised to visit the Pilgrim book and art store of A. S. Burbank. Here you will find a fine collection of choice souvenirs in pictures, china, Pilgrim souvenir spoons and post-cards, also photographs of the Howland homestead and the Howland coat-of-arms. To members of the Howland family living at a distance will be sent, on request, a special illustrated catalogue.

"Were a star quenched on high,
For ages would its light
Still travelling downward from the sky
Shine on our mortal sight.
So, when a great man dies,
For years beyond our ken,
The light he leaves behind
Shines on the paths of men."

GENEALOGICAL NOTES AND QUERIES.

A recent dispatch from Turners Falls, Vt., says: — "Mr. John A. Shebell of Riverside, who has been a resident of Gill for more than half a century, recently purchased the Howland house and farm at Riverside, which has been owned by the Howland family since 1736, 174 years. In tearing down a partition, a few days ago, Mr. Shebell found a shot bag and in the bag were silver coins." Does any one know which branch of the Howland family settled in Turners Falls, Vt.?

PERSONAL.

The thanks of all Howland descendants are due to Mr. John Crocker Foote of Belvidere, Illinois, who has been the largest contributor to the Howland House Fund, and it has been largely due to his liberality and that of members of his family that it has been possible for the Society to acquire the old Howland house. Mr. Foote is a member of the patriotic societies and is widely known for his patriotic spirit and liberality toward all work of this kind.

Mr. Foote is just building a beautiful new house at Belvidere, Ill., very massive in construction, to cost when completed about $30,000. Set in spacious grounds, adorned with large trees, this superb Colonial mansion will be a splendid ornament to East Lincoln Avenue and to the City of Belvidere.

Mr. and Mrs. Summerfield Hagerty of New York, after an interesting trip around the world, are spending the summer at their cottage at Clifton, Mass.

The *Boston Transcript* has become justly celebrated not only for its valuable articles covering a wide range of subjects as well as the news of the day, but its Genealogical Department published twice a week, on Mondays and Wednesdays, offers its columns to those who wish to discover their ancestry, and often an inquiry will supply a "missing link." Write for a free sample copy, which will be sent on application, to the Boston Transcript, 324 Washington Street, Boston, Mass.

Visitors to Plymouth should not fail to visit the "Old Curiosity Shop," to view a collection of curios of the late William Brewster Standish, which is now being rapidly sold.

PRESS OF T. R. MARVIN & SON, BOSTON.

THE HOWLAND HOMESTEAD.

A Magazine to be issued quarterly by the Society of the Descendants of Pilgrim John Howland of the Mayflower. The object of this magazine is to give Howland descendants throughout the world, accurate information about the preservation of the old homestead at Plymouth, personal happenings and general information about the Society. Subscription, $1.00 a year; single copies, 25 cents. Subscribe now and mail a copy to any Howlands you may know. Correspondence solicited and news items about Howland descendants welcomed. Subscribers to the magazine may insert, without charge, genealogical queries in each number, which will be answered as soon as possible. The Personal and Genealogical column will be a feature of the magazine. The editor will attempt to answer all personal letters of inquiry, if such letters contain a self-addressed stamped envelope for reply. Address

Mrs. L. B. TITUS,

Squantum P. O., Quincy, Mass.

The HOWLAND HOMESTEAD.

Vol. 1 BOSTON, OCTOBER, 1911. No. 2

The Howland House, Plymouth, Mass. Built, 1667.

Thanksgiving Number.

Published by the
Society of the Descendants of Pilgrim John Howland, of the Ship "Mayflower."
Office, 6 Beacon Street, Room 908,
Boston.

The Howland Homestead.

Vol. I. BOSTON, MASS., OCTOBER, 1911. No. 2.

"One small candle may light a thousand."

THE success that has attended the publication of the HOWLAND HOMESTEAD has been very gratifying, and the Editor desires to express appreciation for the kind words of encouragement and interest received. The little magazine seems to supply a long-felt want, and makes it possible for members of the Howland family living far from Plymouth to keep in touch with the work the Society is doing not only to preserve and hand down to posterity the last house left standing to-day in Plymouth whose walls have listened to the voices of the Mayflower passengers, and where John Howland and his wife must have often been, but also to furnish accurate information about research work which will soon be undertaken to try to ascertain the ancestry of John Howland in England. It has been found that descendants of Pilgrim John Howland are living in different parts of the world—many particularly are settled in California. We wish to reach every person who claims descent from John and Elizabeth Tilley Howland, and the Editor of this magazine cordially invites you to send the names and addresses of all such persons. Those who are far from Plymouth can help on the work of the restoration of the old home at Plymouth by buying a copy of this Magazine and sending it to any Howland Descendants who might be interested.

You will notice that the photograph shows that to the left of the house, in fact only twenty feet from it, is a livery stable, which stands on part of the original Howland lot. It greatly increases the danger of fire and should be removed. The owner offers to sell it to the Society for a reasonable sum. If the stable could be torn down, and a beautiful lawn graded and set with old-fashioned shrubs and flowers, it would add greatly to the Homestead. Will not some of our Howland Descendants start a fund for the removal of the stable and for the necessary work? About $2,000 will be needed. As soon as the deed of the house is in the possession of the Society, the next work must be to restore the house to the style of the colonial days and remove the stable. We ask your help—to interest any Howland Descendants you may know. Letters of inquiry should contain a self-addressed envelope for reply.

All persons having any acquaintance with the Howland family in England, or have any original MSS. or any papers relating to the early history of the Howlands, are invited to send them to the Editor for publication in the magazine. Address all communications to

MRS. NELSON V. TITUS, *Secretary and Treasurer*,
Squantum P. O., Quincy, Mass.,
or 6 Beacon St., Boston. Room 908.

ANNUAL MEETING.

The Annual Meeting of the Society of the Descendants of Pilgrim John Howland of the Ship "Mayflower" was held at the Samoset House, Plymouth, Saturday, Sept. 2, 1911, with a full attendance of members and friends. The President, Mr. C. S. Ward, presided. The first business was to complete the Articles of Incorporation of the Society. The Secretary's report showed that during the past year 16 persons had joined the society. Seven persons also joined the society at this meeting. Much business relating to the purchase of the old house was transacted. Before the business meeting the members of the society went to the grave of John Howland on Burial Hill, as is the annual custom, and there placed a large laurel wreath. The Church and the old House on Sandwich Street were also visited. Dinner was served at the Samoset House at 2 P. M. Miss Helen R. Holmes, the owner of the old Howland House, was the guest of honor at the dinner. Other guests present were President and Mrs. H. B. Hutchins of Ann Arbor, Mich. After dinner, Mr. William A. Howland of Ann Arbor, Mich., gave a fine rendering of his original composition set to the words of Mrs. Heman's famous poem, "The Breaking Waves Dashed High," which was greatly enjoyed. The exercises closed by all singing "America," after which an opportunity was given to meet Miss Holmes. At the business meeting the following officers were elected by ballot to serve the Society for 1911-12.

President, Mr. CLARENCE S. WARD, Boston.
Vice President, Rear Admiral GEORGE C. REMEY, Washington, D. C.
Secretary and Treasurer, Mrs. L. B. TITUS.

Executive Committee

Miss ANNIE K. WILSON, West Haven, Conn.
Miss G. M. PRUE, Boston.
Miss M. E. KNOWLES, Providence, R. I.
Mrs. E. S. BURNHAM, Portland, Me.

It was the sentiment of all present that the meeting had been most enjoyable, and all hoped to be present at the next annual meeting at the same place in September, 1912.

NEW MEMBERS.

Since our last issue the following descendants of John Howland have joined the Society:—

Major Carver Howland, U. S. A.
Mr. Edward F. Weed.
Mrs. Sam'l R. Weed.
Miss Ellen Huldah Newton.
Miss C. Augusta Cobb.
Mrs. Elizabeth Howland Pitman.
Mrs. James Walter Heustis.
Mrs. H. B. Hutchins.
Mrs. George L. Munn.
Mrs. Helen M. Wallace.
Mrs. L. S. Johnson.

THE ANCESTRY OF JOHN HOWLAND OF THE "MAYFLOWER."

Since the death of Colonel Chester, the barrister and noted antiquary of England, who prosecuted a search to ascertain the ancestry of John Howland in England, nothing has been done to follow up the clues obtained by Colonel Chester.

New interest has, however, been revived to prosecute the search by an offer recently made by a prominent genealogist in England. He offers to find the ancestry of John Howland. If he succeeds he is to receive $500, if he does not succeed he is to receive no pay. This seems to be a fair proposition, and as there are many of the Howland descendants in America who wish to trace their ancestry in England, the editor of this magazine offers its columns for any discussion or advice upon the subject and will receive subscriptions. No money need be sent until the whole amount is subscribed. The following amount has been subscribed and other subscriptions will be duly acknowledged in the HOMESTEAD.

Howland Research Fund.

Mr. L. M. Howland, Paris $20.00

When Colonel Chester investigated the records of the Howland family in England in 1879, he found that all of the name traced back to the County of Essex, England, but subsequent researches have proved that many of the name lived and died in other counties.

Meadows Cowper, an authority on Kentist Genealogy, asserts that the name Howland is synonymous with :—

Houghlyn:	will of	John Houghlyn	dated	5 April, 1452.
Howlyng:	" "	Henry Howlyng	"	21 December, 1479.
Howghlin:	" "	William Howghlin	"	5 June, 1497.
Howlyn:	" "	William Howlyn	"	3 February, 1498–9.
Hughlyn:	" "	Walter Hughlyn	"	5 October, 1513.
Howlyn:	" "	Thomas Howlyn	"	3 May, 1521.
Howlen:	" "	Simon Howlen	"	22 January, 1522.
Howlend:	" "	Simon Howlend	"	18 April, 1517.
Howlynn:	" "	Hamond Howlynn	"	1 June 1542.
Howlinge:	" "	Thomas Howlings	"	13 September, 1557.
Howllin:	" "	Symon Howllen	"	20 August, 1600.
Howland:	" "	Alexander Howland	"	10 February, 1608.
Howlin:	" "	Stephen Howlin	"	22 January, 1623.

Howline (Ursula)	baptized	19 March, 1610.
Howllande, James	"	7 March, 1597–80.
Howllen, Joan	"	2 February, 1580–1.
Howling (Thomarzine)	buried	11 March, 1585–6.
Howlinne (Robert)	baptized	27 October, 1588.
Howllyn (Elizabeth)	"	15 September, 1595.

Certain it is, that on the Bishop's Transcripts of Canterbury, for the town of Mersham, we find :—

12 April, 1619, John son of Robert Howland buried:

16 January, 1619–20 Mary daughter of Robert Howlin baptized: undoubtedly children of the same Robert.

It is regrettable that no trace of the Pilgrim Howlands were found among the records at Canterbury. A remarkable coincidence in names, as in the Pilgrim family, is found in the will of a certain Symon Howllen (of Smeeth, Kent), dated 20 August, 1600.

He mentions brother Christopher,
son Stephen,
son John,
son Henry,
son (Jesper),
grandson John, son of Henry,
" George, " " "
six grandchildren (unnamed), children of Stephen,
daughter Ann Andrewe,
Susan, wife of son Jesper,
Mary, " " " Stephen,
Ursula, " " " John.

Humphrey Howland mentions in his will his brothers, Arthur, John and Henry, also sister Margaret Philipps, and nephew and niece Simon and Hanna.

In Symon Howllen's will we have the familiar names of John and Henry and Simon, but they are not our people as,—

John, son of Symon Howllen, was married before September, 1600, when John, the Pilgrim, was only eight years old, and the will does not mention Arthur Howland, born in 1588, Humphrey, George or Margaret. Researches made in Kent have produced no clue as yet to the ancestry of the American Howland Pilgrim, but the following Latin translation of an Inquisition of 1333, relating to a certain **Robert de Houland** and his wife Maud, is interesting, and also extracts from a Latin document in the Record office, London (1323–1324), which mentions **Maud Moubray**, daughter of Robert de Houlande, is probably the same as the above. Genealogists in England think that Houland is Howland. The name Houland is of Saxon origin, but as w and u were used interchangeably in many old documents it is fair to presume that the name is the same.

EXTRACTS, translated from a Latin document in the Record office, London.

From the Account of the Constable of The Tower of London. Exchequer Queen's Remembrancer Accounts, Army, etc.

17–18 Edward II (1323–1324).

PRISONERS, He renders an account of the prisoners received from W. Bishop of Exeter and Treasurer of England, to wit,

Roger de Mortimer,	John Deyuile,
John de la Beche,	Richard de Ideshale,
Thomas de Gournay,	Walter de Selebi,
John le Fitz Simond,	Giles de Badelesmere,
Edmund Darel,	Geoffrey de la Mare,
Hugh Deyland,	John Queynte,
John de Vaus,	John Burel,
Bartholemew de Borgheraisse,	John Page,

Richard Bullok,	Joan Dausti, her handmaid,
Elizabeth de Borgheraisse,	John de Lancaster,
Giles de Borgheraisse,	William de Benham,
John de Moubray,	John de Bokynham,
Richard de Pesehale,	Robert de Stanford,
Maud de Moubray,	

John de Holebroke, who was with Lady de Badelesmere.

Total: 27 persons, of these persons he renders account as follows:—

ITEM, he renders account of the delivery of Maud Moubray, daughter of Robert de Houlonde, by the King's writ in these words:

Edward by the Grace of God King of England, Lord of Ireland and Duke of Aquitaine, to our well-beloved and trusty John de Wetstone, Constable of our Tower of London, greeting. We command you to deliver the daughter of Robert de Houlande, who is in your custody in our said Tower, to our well-beloved clerk Richard de Lusteshulle, warden of the Hospital of St. Katherine beside our said Tower, or to his lieutenant there, to be kept according as we command him by our other letters, and whom we have commanded to receive her from you. And we will that this letter shall be your warrant. Given under our privy seal at Westminster on the 28th day of May in the seventeenth year of our reign (1324).

ITEM, he renders account of the delivery of Joan Austy, handmaid of the said Maud de Houlande, by the King's writ in these words:

Edward by the Grace of God King of England, Lord of Ireland and Duke of Aquitaine, to his well-beloved and trusty John Wetstone, Constable of our Tower of London, greeting. We command you to deliver from the same Tower Joan Austy, damsel, who was serving the wife of the late John de Moubrai, our enemy and rebel, and who is in our prison in the Tower aforesaid, if she is in our prison aforesaid because she served the aforenamed wife of the said John, and not for any other reason. Witness myself at Westminster on the first day of June in the seventeenth year (1324).

Total of persons delivered 15

And there remain 12 persons, to wit,

Roger de Mortimer, Richard de Ideshale, John de la Beche, Walter de Selby, Bartholemew de Burgheraisse, Giles de Badelesmere, John de Benham, John de Moubray, Elizabeth de Borgheraise, John de Vaus, Richard Bullok, John de Holebroke, who was in the custody of Lady de Baldelesmere.

Total: 12 persons remaining in the Tower of London, for whom he must answer next year. And he answers as appears there.

18th year (1324–5)

He renders account of the prisoners remaining in the Tower last year (as above).

Total 12 persons;

He accounts for the delivery of John, son of John de Mowbray(sic) by the King's writ in these words: Edward by the Grace of God King of England, Lord of Ireland and Duke of Ireland, to our well-beloved and trusty John de Westone, Constable of our Tower of London, greeting. We command you on sight of these letters to deliver John, son of John de Moubray, a prisoner in your custody in our Tower, to Richard de Pesehale, bearer thereof to bring him to our dear nephew, our trusty Hugh le Despenser the son, to whom we have given the body of the said John. And we will that this letter shall be your warrant for the same. Given under our privy seal at Henley on the 8th day of August in the 18th year of our reign (1324), *John de Vauux, Richard Bullok, John de Holebroke, prisoners aforesaid were sent to Westminster to appear before G de Scrope, Justice of the Lord King before whom they were delivered.* Note. The words in italics above, are crossed out in the original, because the warrant is wanting.

I

II Total 4

And there remain 8 prisoners to wit,
Roger de Mortimer, Richard de Ideshale, John de la Beche, Walter de Selby, Bartholomew de Borgheraisse, Giles de Badelesmere, John de Benham, Elizabeth de Borgheraisse.
Total 8 persons. And he must further answer for the bodies of the said John de Vaus, Richard Bullok and John de Holebroke, whom he says he delivered as above in the lines in italics, because he shows no warrant.

NOTE. It is interesting to note that Stowe's Annals, under the year 1325 reports that: "On Lammas day Roger Mortimer of Wigmore, by making a solemn banquet to Sir Stephen Segrave, Constable of the Tower of London, and the other officers, and giving to his keepers a sleepe drink, escaped out of the Tower, breaking through the wall, and coming into the kitchen neere adjoyning to the King's lodgings, and getting out of the toppe thereof, came unto a warde of the Tower, and so with the cordes knit ladder-wise prepared aforehand by a friend of his, got to another warde, and so with greate feare got to the Thamis, and with his helper and two mo of his counsell passed the river, and avoiding the high waies came to the sea, and there finding a shippe at Porchester, he passed ouer into France to the King there, where he lived long, looking when he might be reconciled to the King of England; his uncle Roger being stil kept in filthy prison the space almost of fiue years very uncourteously; at length he died, and was buried at Bristowe; for the escape of the yoonger Mortimer, the King being sore offended, put Sir Stephen Segrave out of his Constableshp of the Tower."

The Hospital of St. Katherine by the Tower was founded by Mathilda, wife to King Stephen, by license from the Prior and Convent of the Holy Trinity in London, on whose ground she founded it in the year 1140. It was refounded by Queen Eleanor, wife of Edward I, and she appointed here a Master, three brethren, ten poor women, and six poor clerks.

EMELINA LONGESPEE.

Inquisition taken at New Salisbury, before Edward Selyman the King's escheator, 22d February, 7 Edward III (1333) by the oath of Robert de Horput, John Fyzwilliam, John de Blake, Thomas Dygon, John Saucer, John le Palmere, John att Brugge, John de Wyke, Robert le Nywe, Thomas Chepman, Adam Cook, and William Herberd, who say that
Emelina Longesepee held nothing of the King in chief in Wilts but she held for the term of her life on the day she died the Manor of Wambergh (excepting 10 pounds worth of land in the same Manor) from John Warren, Earl of Surrey, as of the Lordship of the earldom of Salisbury (Salisbury) by the service of one knight's fee. It is worth 40 pounds, in addition to the said 10 pounds. The said Emelina died on Whit-Sunday, 5 Edward III (1331). The Manor (except the 10 pounds worth) ought to remain to Maud, formerly wife of Robert de Houland, by fine levied in the King's court, 7 Edward II (1313–14) between the said Emelina and Hugh de Denford (Denford), who was then seized of that Manor. It was thereby conveyed to the said Emelina for life, remainder to Thomas, late Earl of Lancaster, for life, remainder to Robert de Houland and Maud his wife, and the heirs of the said Maud for ever.
One William Fortel held to him and his heirs a moiety of the Manor of Stepellanynton by demise of the said Emelina, paying her 10 pounds for the whole of her life (sic).
Maud, formerly wife of the said Robert de Houland, and Ellen her sister, are the next heirs of the said Emelina, and are aged 40 and more.

Chan. Inq. P. M. Ser. I. 6 Edward III, Ist Nos., No. 43.
New reference, Chan. Inq. p. m. Edward III, file 32. No. 2.

THE OLD HOWLAND HOUSE.

"Solid, substantial, of timber
Rough-hewn from the firs of the forest." —*Longfellow.*

The old Howland house was erected by Jacob Mitchell, probably between 1665 and 1670, as he married in 1666 and bought the lot in 1667. He sold it to Jabez Howland undoubtedly before John Howland's death. The main room of the old house remains in nearly its original condition, and if its walls could speak, they would repeat the words of John and his wife Elizabeth.

The furnishing of four rooms has been promised by the following persons: Mr. John Crocker Foote of Belvidere, Ill., will furnish the living room in memory of his mother, Mrs. Mary Crocker Foote; Mrs. Summerfield Hagerty will furnish another room in memory of her grandmother, Mrs. Dorcas Gardner Swift, a descendant of John Howland in the Gardner line. Mrs. Lucy E. Wallace and her cousin, Mrs. Lillie B. Titus, will furnish another room in memory of their grandfather, Captain James Huckins, a descendant through Thomas Huckins of Barnstable from Hope Howland, a daughter of John Howland of the "Mayflower." Mrs. Mary S. Burnham of Portland, Me., will also furnish a room. As the house contains but 10 rooms, two of which must be reserved for the caretaker, it will be seen that there are but four rooms remaining, so that early application is necessary to secure one. The rooms are small and require little furniture.

For further information address the Secretary, Mrs. L. B. Titus.

PERSONAL.

One of the prettiest home weddings of the season took place on Saturday evening, October 14th, when the beautiful summer cottage of Mr. and Mrs. Summerfield Hagerty of New York, on Gun Rock Point, Clifton, Mass., was bright with music and flowers for the marriage of the daughter of Mrs. Hagerty, Miss Mary Phillips Stran to Mr. Henry Lewis Appleton of Philadelphia, Pa. The bride looked charming in a beautiful gown of white crêpe de Chine embroidered in silver, wrought in the "Queen Mary" pattern, which was noticeably beautiful; only one other gown like it ever having been made. It was purchased by the bride on her recent visit to Delhi, India. She carried a shower bouquet of lilies of the valley and was attended by the maid of honor, Miss Gladys Weaver of Baltimore, whose gown was of pink satin with white tulle. The five bridesmaids were Miss Mary Bair, Philadelphia, Pa., Miss Edith Schonberger, Philadelphia, Pa., Miss Emily Barnum, Chicago, Miss Helen Hagerty, Baltimore, Miss Frances McLellan, Boston. These ladies wore light pink silk gowns.

The mother of the bride, Mrs. Summerfield Hagerty, looking as youthful as her daughter, wore a beautiful gown of white corded silk with Maltese lace and pearl jewelry. She carried a bouquet of pink roses. Among the guests noted were Mr. John L. Appleton, the father of the groom, from Philadelphia, and many guests from New York, Boston, Philadelphia and Baltimore.

The presents were noticeably beautiful and filled one entire room in the house. The supper was served by E. P. Cassell, the well-known colored caterer of Salem, and the Salem Cadet Band furnished the music.

After a wedding trip to Montreal and Quebec, Mr. and Mrs. Appleton will be at home to their many friends at No. 3312 Hamilton St., Philadelphia, Pa.

OUR LONG-LOST ANCESTOR.

I had a Howland grandfather and was early taught that I was descended from John Howland of the "Mayflower" and his wife Elizabeth, daughter of Governor Carver. This tradition had been handed down in an unbroken line in the different branches of the Howland family. Indeed it was more than tradition, for Belknap, Thatcher and Prince mentioned it as an historical fact. It was therefore a great shock when "Bradford's Journal" was discovered to find it therein stated that John Howland married Elizabeth Tilley. It was not easy to accept and reconcile this with our former belief, so much controversy followed, and it was questioned whether John Howland could have been twice married.

When it was announced in the "Hartford Times" that a "Mayflower" Bible had been found containing records in which Brewster, Bradford, White and Howland were mentioned I lost no time in seeking its owner. I found him, Mr. Cowles, a genial old gentleman, and when I made known my errand he said I might see the Bible if I would handle it carefully as it was very old. Undoubtedly it was very old, this curious square volume, for it not only contained the Bible, including the Apocrypha and Commentary, but preceding it was the book of Common Prayer and following it was Steinhold and Hopkins' version of the Psalms. It was printed in black letter in 1586. Together we sat on the porch searching for the records which Mr. Cowles could not remember. We found many on the margins in the book of Common Prayer, none in the Bible. Under a little pen picture of a ship was written William White, his book 1619; later was recorded the marriage of William White to Susannah Fuller, and upon another margin the birth of Peregrine White on board the "Mayflower" in Cape Cod harbor. There were many other records too numerous for the limits of this article, but what to me was of the greatest interest was this writing:—

"John Howland married Katharaine Tilley, granddarter of John Carver, Govener of Plymouth, appointed anno domino 16, now called New Plymouth."

This seemed a solution of the vexed question, the granddaughter instead of daughter of John Carver, and probably she held the place of a daughter in the family. We know that her name was Elizabeth not Katharaine. Mrs. Carver's name was Katharine, but the inaccuracy might be accounted for in various ways.

The next question was the history of the Bible. Who could prove the genuineness of the many records therein, that was a mystery.

Mr. Cowles had bought the Bible a few years previous from a teacher in Manchester, Conn., a Mr. Taintor, who had sold it with a few dollars in exchange for Peter Parley's "Recollections of a Life Time." Mr. Taintor had spoken apologetically of some scribblings in the book but Mr. Cowles had never taken the trouble to look at them.

In September, 1894, the "Hartford Times" published an account of a curious old Bible known as the Breeches Bible, then Mr. Cowles carried his book to the "Times" office for inspection. Mr. Frank Burr, the editor, a man of great learning, was surprised to find records which convinced him the book was brought over in the "Mayflower" and published a long article concerning it.

I inquired of Mr. Cowles where Mr. Taintor had found the Bible and he said that some time after he had bought it he drove to Manchester to find out but learned that Mr. Taintor had died, and his father did not know anything of its history, there was only an impression of "somewhere up the river."

When one critic said the records could not be genuine as it was not the "writing of that period," I determined to know what was the writing of the period, so examined old records in Salem, Boston and Plymouth, letter by letter, and was pleased to learn that not only was it the writing of that time, but that the Bible contained genuine autographs of William Brewster. After the death of William White, which occurred early in the history of the colony, the book became the property of Elder William Brewster, given by Susannah White. His name is written in several places; one signature has under it Emanuel College, England. The signature is singularly like one on a pamphlet printed by Brewster in Leyden and is now in Yale College library,—it has also been proved that Brewster went to Emanuel College, Cambridge, England.

Much more might be told of other records, and funny scribblings on fly leaves, pen pictures of Indians, log houses, a cradle under which is printed "oceanicus," and a small meeting house quite like the earliest of New England houses of worship.

Mr. Cowles did not wish to sell the Bible nor did he claim that it was a Mayflower Bible until Mr. Burr told him what he had found. When I asked if he had ever heard of the Carver-Tilley controversy or of John Howland he replied, "I never heard of the man." The records seemed to form a sort of diary and evidently were written by several different persons.

When the "Bradford Journal" was discovered, the John Howland descendants gave up with much regret their honored and cherished ancestor Governor Carver. It is with the hope that he may be restored to us the above article is penned.

ALICE HOWLAND GOODWIN.

"Help one another," the snowflakes said,
As they cuddled down in their fleecy bed.
"One of us here would not be felt,
One of us there would quickly melt;
But I'll help you, and you help me,
And then what a splendid drift there'll be."

We regret to note the death of a member of the Society, Mr. Walter Morton Howland, at his residence in East Amherst, Mass. Mr. Howland was greatly interested in genealogical matters and was formerly Governor of the Society of Mayflower Descendants in the state of Illinois, during his residence in Chicago. He was lately Treasurer of Amherst College.

THE WIDOW GRAY'S THANKSGIVING.

(A True Story.)

Old and poor sat the Widow Gray
At her cottage door in the fading light,
Gazing sadly out into the night
On the evening before Thanksgiving Day
In Plymouth down by the sea.

Three long years have passed away
Since the widow's son, her pride and joy,
Started away from Boston Bay
To sail for the Indies hoping to make
A fortune there for his mother's sake.

But the years have come and the years have gone
While she lives there neglected and all alone,
And sorrow and want have come to stay
In the humble home of the Widow Gray.
For no news has come from day to day
From the good Ship "Rover" far away.
So the neighbors sigh and whisper low
When they meet at the Deacon's quilting bee,
"Poor Mrs. Gray! she's got to go
Soon to the poorhouse on the hill,
There's no one to help her that can or will!"
Then up in her place rose Bessie Lee
With a light in her eyes that was good to see,
The prettiest girl in all the town
From her dainty feet to her ringlets brown,
The fair young daughter of Deacon Lee
In Plymouth down by the sea.

"Now neighbors and friends, full well I know
Ye all feel sorry for Mrs. Gray,
Perhaps to the poorhouse she may go
But I'd like to give her one happy day.
Now from house to house I'll gladly go
If each of you'll give me some little thing,
I'm sure to us all 'twill a blessing bring!
Now neighbors and friends, what do you say?
Shall we give her one happy Thanksgiving Day?"

Thanksgiving morn rose dark and chill,
A thick fog settled on sea and shore
And the air was heavy and cold and still,
But undeterred by the dreary day
Fair Bessie hastened on her way
To the humble home of the Widow Gray.
Her willing hands the carpet swept,
The fire kindled, the kettle filled,

Her basket full of wholesome things,
The jars of honey, the cakes and pies
Unpacked to the widow's eager eyes.
"God bless you, Lassie!" the old dame said
As she tenderly stroked that curly head,
"May your life be always fair and bright,
May your purse be heavy, your heart be light
And good fortune attend your steps alway
For the comfort you've brought to Matilda Gray."
The snow was falling fast without,
The wind went whistling down the street
They did not hear the noise about
The neighing horse, the tramp of feet,
Until at the door a hearty shout
Startled the people roundabout.
Pale with fear rose the Widow Gray.
"Have they come to take me?" she faintly says.
"No, no," said Bessie, "have no fear,
They shall not take you while I am here!"
But now at the door is heard a voice
That makes that mother's heart rejoice.
"Open the door. It's I, it's Tom!
Oh, mother, mother; at last I'm home!"
He flings it wide, and to his heart
Clasps the dear old face, so pale and worn,
While Bessie silently steals away
To scatter the news about the town.
No need to tell of young Captain Gray
With his good ship "Rover" safe in port,
Arriving back into Boston Bay
Just on the eve of Thanksgiving Day.
Forgetting all else in his joy and pride
He mounts a horse and away he rides
To carry the news of his safe return
And to see his dear old mother at home
In Plymouth down by the sea.
My tale is told but the papers say,
There was a wedding next Thanksgiving Day
In the fine new house on the shore of the Bay
When Bessie Lee was made Bessie Gray,
In Plymouth down by the sea.

LILLIE B. TITUS.

PLYMOUTH ROCK.

"That great gray Rock, itself a Pilgrim as has been well said, from some far northern shore, brought here by the vast forces of nature and laid to wait in grand patience, until the ages should bring it a name, a use, and a nation's love and honor."

JANE AUSTEN.

CONTRIBUTORS TO THE FUND FOR THE PRESERVATION OF THE OLD HOWLAND HOUSE AT PLYMOUTH, MASS.

The last house left standing to-day in Plymouth whose walls have listened to the voices of the Mayflower Pilgrims.

Mrs. Mary P. Hagerty.
Mrs. Lucy E. Wallace.
Mr. John Crocker Foote.
Mr. Charles Howland Russell.
Miss Mary A. Sharpe.
Mrs. Samuel S. Spaulding.
Mrs. Simeon B. Chittenden.
Hon. Seth Low.
Miss Mary E. Knowles.
Mr. Charles E. Sherman.
Master John Howland Yates.
Mrs. Frederick Allien.
Mr. Ellis B. Usher.
"A Friend."
Mrs. A. Louise Williams.
Miss M. L. Williams.
Mr. & Mrs. Charles H. Warren.
Miss Grace M. Prue.
Mr. Cyrus Woodman.
Mrs. James L. Morgan.
Dr. Samuel F. Howland.
Miss Caroline C. Shaw.
Mrs. G. Wilbur Smith.
Miss Mary Woodman.
Mrs. Arthur W. Howe.
Mr. William B. Howland.
Mr. L. M. Howland.
Mrs. Enos Clarke.
Miss M. Louise Greene.
Mrs. Harriet Foote Sabin.
In memory of
Mr. Abiah Jenkins Hine.
Hollingsworth Hine (s).
Mrs. Ruth Howland Hall.
In memory of
Joseph W. Hines.
Mrs. Marcella Hall Hines (his wife).
Mr. Edward M. Hines.
Miss Marcella M. Hines.
Miss Ada C. H. Stoddard.
Miss Ava M. Stoddard.
Miss Edna D. Stoddard.
Mrs. Ella H. Stratton.
Mr. Ray H. Stratton.
Miss Jeanette M. Stratton.
Miss Josephine W. Stratton.
Miss Kate Irish.
Mr. Gilbert Irish.
Albion W. Stratton.
Mr. James S. Burke.
Rev. Alfred Gooding.
Mr. John M. Stevenson.
Mrs. Luther S. Johnson.
Mr. William I. Wardwell.
Mr. O. A. Day.
Mr. Henry E. Howland.
Mrs. S. D. Merrill.
Miss Addie M. Howland.
Mr. Charles Perry.
Mrs. Alice S. Stone.
Miss Elsa W. Stone.
Miss Emma Warren.
Admiral G. C. Remey, U. S. N.
Mrs. Charles F. Cadle.
Mr. Henry R. Howland.
Miss Mary A. Sharpe.
Mrs. Helen M. Wallace.
Mrs. Laura Lee Armstrong.
Mrs. Alice Howland Goodwin.

Further subscriptions are earnestly requested in order that the work of restoration of the old house to the style of the colonial days may be begun in the spring. It is estimated that it will cost at least $2,000 to restore the house to the style of the colonial days, in addition to what must be paid to purchase and tear down the unsightly stable, which is a constant menace to the old house as will be seen by the photograph.

SOCIETY OF THE DESCENDANTS OF PILGRIM JOHN HOWLAND OF THE SHIP "MAYFLOWER."

OFFICERS.

President, Mr. CLARENCE STUART WARD, Boston.
Vice President, Rear Admiral GEORGE C. REMEY, U. S. N., Washington, D. C.
Secretary and Treasurer, Mrs. NELSON V. TITUS, Squantum, Quincy, Mass.

This Society was organized at Plymouth, Mass., May 18, 1897, for the following purposes:—

"To perpetuate the memory of our ancestors, John Howland and his wife, Elizabeth Tilley, who, braving the perils of the deep, were among that little band of Pilgrims who landed from the Ship 'Mayflower' on Plymouth Rock, Dec. 21, 1620; to preserve and publish any manuscript relating to the families of John Howland and his wife, to erect and keep in good repair a memorial to their memory in the Pilgrim Church at Plymouth, to assist in prosecuting research in England and Holland to discover their ancestry; to preserve and if possible acquire possession of the Howland House in Plymouth, and to endeavor to acquire a better knowledge of the causes which led them to emigrate to the new world."

The Memorial Pulpit to our ancestors has been placed in the Pilgrim Church at Plymouth, and a silver tablet upon it states that it is the gift of the descendants of John Howland.

The work now undertaken is the acquisition and preservation by the Society of the Howland House in Plymouth, built in 1667.

As many descendants of John Howland live in distant parts of the country and cannot attend meetings, the entrance fee to the Society has been placed at $1.00 with annual dues of but $1.00 a year, to cover postage and printing. Life membership $20.00.

If the old house is secured by this Society it is probable that the annual meeting of the Society will be held there each summer.

You are cordially invited to join the Society, which seeks to unite all descendants of the "Beloved Pilgrim" in all parts of our land. Please extend this invitation to any descendants of John Howland whom you may know. Application blanks will be furnished, and any further information will be given by addressing the Secretary.

THE HOWLAND HOMESTEAD.

A Magazine to be issued quarterly by the Society of the Descendants of Pilgrim John Howland of the Mayflower. The object of this magazine is to give Howland descendants throughout the world, accurate information about the preservation of the old homestead at Plymouth, personal happenings and general information about the Society. Subscription, $1.00 a year; single copies, 25 cents. Subscribe now and mail a copy to any Howlands you may know. Correspondence solicited and news items about Howland descendants welcomed. Subscribers to the magazine may insert, without charge, genealogical queries in each number, which will be answered as soon as possible. The Personal and Genealogical column will be a feature of the magazine. The editor will attempt to answer all personal letters of inquiry, if such letters contain a self-addressed stamped envelope for reply. Address

Mrs. L. B. TITUS,
Squantum P. O., Quincy, Mass.

The
HOWLAND HOMESTEAD

Vol. 1. BOSTON, MASS., APRIL, 1912. No. 3.

The Howland House, Plymouth, Mass. Built 1667.

Published by the

Society of the Descendants of Pilgrim John Howland, of the Ship "Mayflower"

Office, 6 Beacon Street, Room 908

Boston.

The Howland Homestead.

Vol. I. BOSTON, MASS., APRIL, 1912 No. 3

"One small candle may light a thousand."

OWING to unexpected delays the April number of the Homestead will be substituted for the number which should have been issued in January, and with the July number, now in press, will complete Vol. 1 of the magazine.

It is with great pleasure that we are able to announce that the July number will contain a most interesting article, entitled "John Howland, a Mayflower Pilgrim," by Mr. Henry R. Howland, who has for years been collecting for publications all that can be learned of our ancestor, John Howland.

This edition is limited so early application should be made for extra copies if desired.

We are also pleased to announce that a deed of the old Howland House on Sandwich Street, Plymouth, has now been secured by the Society. The house in its present condition is uninhabitable and extensive repairs are needed at once in order that a caretaker may be installed in the house and it may be opened to visitors.

Once restored the house will be self supporting. There will be no taxes to pay, as, owing to a recent decision of the Supreme Court, such old houses in Massachusetts that are kept for historical purposes are exempt from taxation.

The old stable, which is a constant fire menace, being but 20 feet from the old house, should be purchased by the Society and torn down. Members are asked to examine the photograph closely and note existing conditions. If the stable could be removed and a lawn graded with old-fashioned flowers it would add greatly to the Homestead. To accomplish all this at least $5000 is needed. Is it not possible to raise this sum to preserve and hand down to posterity the last house left standing today in Plymouth whose walls have listened to the voices of the Mayflower Pilgrims? Who will help complete this patriotic work? One thousand dollars has already been subscribed. The names of all donors will be placed on a tablet in the house to be forever preserved. Subscriptions should be sent to

Mrs. L. B. Titus, *Secretary and Treasurer,*
Squantum P.O. Quincy, Mass.

The Will of Elizabeth (Tilley) Howland

From Original Records, Bristol County, Mass. Probate Records: Vol I, Pages 13 and 14

Elizabeth Tilley Howland, the widow of Pilgrim John Howland, and daughter of John Tilley, died at the home of her daughter, Lydia Brown, the wife of James Brown, at Swansea, Mass., Wednesday, 21 | 31 Dec. 1687. The place of her burial is in doubt. There are no records of early burials at Swansea. It has always been supposed that she was buried there, but Sept. 5th last, when the Society of the Descendants of Pilgrim John Howland visited Burial Hill attention was called to the old footstone at the grave of Pilgrim John Howland half buried in the grass. This bears the initials "J. H. E. H." The supposition, therefore, arises that Mrs. Howland was buried in the same grave with her husband. Accurate information on this matter is greatly desired. The will is as follows:

In Y^e^ name of God Amen I Elizabeth Howland of Swanzey in ye county of Bristoll in Y Collony of Plymouth in New Eng being Seventy nine yeares of Age but of good & perfect memory thanks be to Allmighty God & calling to Remembrance ye uncertain Estate of this transitory life & that all flesh must Yeild unto Death when it shall please God to call Doe make constitute & ordaine & Declare This my last Will & Testament, in manner & forme following Revoking and Annulling by these p^r^snts all and Every Testam^t^ and Testam^ts^ Will and Wills heretofore by me made & declared Either by Word or Writing And this is to be taken only for my last Will & Testament & none other

And first being penitent & sorry from ye bottom of my heart for all my sinns past and most humbly desiring forgiveness for ye same I give & Comitt my soule unto Allmighty God my Saviour & Redeemer in whom & by y meritts of Jesus Christ I trust and believe assuredly to be saved & to have full remission & forgivenesse of all my sins & that My Soule w^t^ my Body at the generall Day of Resurrection shall rise again w^t^ Joy & through ye meritts of Christ's Death & passion possess & inheritt ye Kingdome of heaven prepared for his Elect& Chosen & my Body to be buryed in such place where it shall please my Execut^r^s hereafter named to appoint and now for ye settling of my temporall Estate & such goodes Chattells & Debts as it hath pleased God far above my Deserts to bestow upon me I Do Dispose order & give ye same in manner & forme following (That is to say) First that after my funerall Expences & Debts paid we I owe either of right or in Conscience to any manner of person or persons whatsoever in Convenient Tyme after my Decease by my Exec^r^s hereafter named I give & bequeath unto my eldest son John Howland ye sum of Five pounds to be paid out of my Estate & my Booke called Mr Tindale's Workes & also one pair of sheetes & one p^r^ of pillowbeeres & one p^r^ of Bedblankettes, Item I give unto my son Joseph Howland my stillyards & also one p^r^ of sheetes & one p^r^ of pillobeeres Item I give unto my son Jabez Howland my ffetherbed & boulster y^t^ is in his Custody & also one Rugg and two Blanketts y^t^ belongeth to ye said Bed & also my great Iron Pot & potthooks Item I give unto my son Isaack Howland my Booke called Willson on ye Romans & one p of sheets & one paire of pillowbeeres & also my great Brasse Kettle already in his possession Item I give unto my Son in Law

Mr James Browne my great Bible Item I give and bequeath unto my Daughtes Lidia Browne my best ffether-bed & Boulster two pillowes & three Blanketts & a green Rugg & my small Cupboard one p^{r} of Andy Irons & my lesser brasr Kettle & my small Bible & my booke of Mr Robbinsons Workes called Observations Divine & Morrall & also my finest p^{r} of Sheetes & my holland pillowbeeres Item I give unto my Daughter Elisabeth Dickensen one p^{r} of sheetes & one p$_{r}$ of pillowbeeres & one Chest. Item I give unto my Daughter Hannah Bosworth one p^{r} of sheets & one p^{r} of pillowbeeres, Item I give unto my Grand Daughter Elizabeth Bursley one paire of sheets and one paire of pillowbeeres Item I give and bequeathe unto my Grandson Nathaniel Howland (the son of Joseph Howland) and to the heires of his owne Body lawfully begotten forever all that my Lott of Land with ye Meadow thereunto adjoining & belonging lying in the Township of Duxbury near Jones River bridge. Item I give unto my Grandson James Browne one Iron Barr and an Iron Trammeli now in his possession Item I give unto my Grandson Jabez Browne one Chest. Item I give unto My Grand Daughter Dorothy Browne my best Chest & my Warming Pan Item I give unto my Grand Daughter Desire Cushman four sheep Item I give & bequeathe my wearing clothes linnen and Woolen and all the rest of my Estate in money Debts linnen of what kind or nature or sort soever it may be unto my three Daughters Elizabeth Dickensen Lidia Browne and Hannah Bosworth to be equally Divided amongst them. Item I make Constitute and ordaine my loving Son in Law James Browne and my loving Son Jabez Howland Executors of this my last Will & Testament. Item it is my Will & Charge to all my children that they walke in ye feare of ye Lord and in Love and peace towards each other and endeavour the true performance of this my last Will & Testament. In Witness Whereof I the said Elizabeth Howland, have hereunto sett my hand & seale this seventeenth Day of December Anno Dm one thousand six hundred Eighty & six.

The mark of Elizabeth E. H. (sigittu)

Signed Sealed and Delivd
in ye presence of us Wittnesses
Hugh Cole
Samuel Vyall
John Browne

Know all men that on ye tenth Day of Janr^{y} Ann^{o} Dm 168 7-8 Before me Nathan Byfield Esqr Judge of his Maj^{ties} Inferiour Court of Pleas for ye County of Bristoll present Jno Walley Esq one of ye members of his Maj^{ties} Councill in New England & Capt. Benjain Church Justice of Peace The above written Will of Elizabeth Howland was proved appointed and allowed And ye Administra^{con} of all & singuler ye goodes Rightes and Creditts of ye said Decd was Committed unto James Browne & Jabez Howland Exec^{rs} in ye same Will named, well & truly to Administer ye same according to the Will of ye Dec^{d}.

In testimony whereof I hereunto Sett ye Seale of y office for Probate of Wills & granting Lett^{rs} of Admin^{con} ye yeare & Day by me above written
(siggittu offici) NATHANIEL BYFIELD

Thus entered & ingrossed this 26: of Jan^{r}y Dm 168 7-8 pr Steph Burton.

No inventory of the personal effects of Mrs. Howland can be found and the original will has also disappeared from the files at the office of the Probate Re cords

The 300th Anniversary of the Landing of the Pilgrims at Plymouth in 1920

AT the Congress of the Society of Mayflower Descendants held at Plymouth, Mass.,Sept. 6,1912,much interest was taken in the various plans proposed for the celebration in 1920 to celebrate the 300th anniversary of the Landing of the Pilgrims. A delegate from the National Society of Colonial Dames, Miss Bissell, of Delaware, stated that she was authorized by her society to pledge the sum of $25,000 to coöperate with other patriotic societies to unite in some grand Memorial to the Pilgrims at Plymouth in 1920.

One plan proposed was to acquire the water front around the Rock, to tear down the unsightly buildings and wharves to make the surroundings around the Rock more appropriate to that "Corner Stone of a Nation."

Another plan is already under way by the Order of Red Men of America. We are informed that an heroic figure of an American Indian in bronze is to be placed on Cole's Hill in memory of Massasoit.

Shall we not have the old Howland House all restored and ready for visitors in 1920? The old house is so near Leyden street that any plans made to improve the water front will bring the old house conspicuously before the eyes of visitors to Plymouth and we should have the house ready and the grounds tastefully laid out before that time.

Much must be done and all Howland Descendants are earnestly asked to seek out other "Howlands." and urge them to unite in thus honoring the memory of our Pilgrim ancestors. If you do not feel you can give much money, try to do what you can. All can give a little time—all can try to seek out other descendants and interest them in the Society. All are cordially invited to coöperate in any way possible in this patriotic work.

Genealogical Queries

Information is greatly desired as to the record of the marriage of Desire Crocker, after the death of her father, Capt. Josiah Crocker, to Grenfell Blake of Taunton, Mass. Where and when were they married? The following is the line desired:

JOHN HOWLAND M ELIZABETH TILLEY

Desire Howland m Capt John Gorham (Ralph) in 1643
Lydia Gorham b 1661 m (sec wife) Col John Thacher (Anthony) Jan 11 1684
Desire Thacher b 1688 m Capt. Josiah Crocker 1718 (Josiah, Dea William)
Desire Crocker b 1721 (after father's death) m Grenfell Blake of Taunton
WHEN & WHERE? M (2) Robert Crossman.
Samuel Blake b 1747 m Abigail Rickard 1768 (Mass Early Marriages)

Anyone having this desired information, please address Mrs. E. H. Stratton, Hopkinton, Mass.

Where is the Grave of Elizabeth Howland, the Wife of the Pilgrim?

WHEN the Society assembled on Burial Hill, Plymouth, on Sept. 5, 1912, much interest was aroused by the discovery of the old footstone at the grave of Pilgrim John Howland. Members of the Society had always supposed that the grave of the Pilgrim faced the west and that the lettering on the stone was on the face of the stone, but the discovery of the old footstone shows that the grave must face the east and the inscription is on the back of the stone.

The inscription on the old footstone, half buried in the grass, of "J. H.-E. H." makes it appear that here also was the last resting place of Elizabeth Howland.

As she died in Swansea it was always supposed that she was there buried. Inquiry of the town clerk of Swansea gives the information that "there is no record of early burials in Swansea."

Where, then, is the grave of Elizabeth Howland?

Can anyone throw any light upon it?

So many inquiries have been made since the publication of the article by Mrs. Joseph Howland in the April "Homestead" about the "new stone" placed through her efforts at the grave of the Pilgrim, that the following article by Mrs. Alice Howland Goodwin about the "old stone," will be of interest:

John Howland's First Headstone

THE story of the first John Howland monument is found in a life of a John Howland of Newport, who was born in 1757. He was afterwards president of the Rhode Island Historical Society, and lived to be over ninety years much beloved and respected.

He was a descendant of the Pilgrim John Howland and it is told that for many years he carefully collected such memorials of his ancestors as records and traditions furnished and entered them into a book. He first went to Plymouth in 1803, made several other visits later. "Sometime between 1824 and 1840 he called upon Dr. Thatcher to search for and identify the grave of John Howland and to superintend the erection of a headstone. They repaired to the registry office to examine early records, and from thence went to the burying ground where the sought-for grave had been identified, went next to the residence of Dr. Le Baron, a gentleman learned in Pilgrim lore, who welcomed Mr. Howland with the warmth of a brother antiquarian. In passing from point to point Dr. Thatcher said, 'I want you to remember everything to which I direct your attention. I am now over ninety years old and shall not be here when you come again.'

"From whence came the tradition? Elder Faunce lived thirty years in Plymouth with the Pillgrim John Howland. Deacon Ephraim Spooner was present when Elder Faunce pointed out the rock as the identical one upon which the Pilgrims landed. He also gave many other traditions.

"In 1803 John Howland of Newport met Deacon Spooner, who was fifty-two years town clerk of Plymouth, and learned much from him concerning the Pilgrims. Dr. Thatcher must also have heard the same.

"By these men the epitaph was prepared and if we accept the story that Elizabeth Tilley was the *granddaughter* of Governor Carver and held the place of a daughter in his home, we can understand how these old men impressed by the fact of kinship should have made the mistake of calling her a daughter. It would certainly seem that such widespread tradition should have some foundation.

ALICE HOWLAND GOODWIN."

Notice

The April number of the Homestead will contain much of interest to Howland Descendents We learn with pleasure, from Miss Elizabeth Howland, that some old letters written by Jabez Howland and his wife Bethaia to which Major Carver Howland, lately deceased, often alluded: are in the possession of her family. It is hoped they may be some day loaned for exhibition in the old Howland House.

All the Howland Descendants are earnestly requested to seek out any articles of furniture, old mirrors anything to help furnish the house. These articles may be loaned, if desired, and will be carefully cared for. Please write the Secretary if you have any articles that you are willing to loan to help furnish the house.

It is expected that the work of restoring the house will be begun in April, and a full account of the restoration of the house will be given in the July Homestead. It is hoped the restoration of the house to the style of the Colonial Days will be completed so that the house may be open for inspection at the Annual Meeting of the Society in September 4, 1913.

Your cordial co-operation and help will be greatly appreciated.

Squantum

On Sept. 30, 1621, Capt. Myles Standish and ten of his men, of whom our ancestor John Howland was one, came into Boston Bay from Plymouth, guided by the Indian Tisquantum they landed on the beach of the Chapel Rocks at Squantum Head. An interesting article will appear shortly in this Magazine, which will be of interest to all Howland Decendants.

What We Call Dying

"We stand upon the seashore in the twilight to watch a stately ship sailing out to sea. As we watch her, she fades away in the distance. We strain our eyes to follow her and at last sadly say 'She has gone!'

"But far away in the East in the glorious morning sunshine a joyous sound arises, and a goodly company exclaim with shouts of welcome, 'Here she comes!"

In Memoriam

We regret to announce the death of a valued member of our Society, Mrs. Enos Clarke, of Kirkwood, Mo., on Oct. 10, 1912. Mrs. Clarke was one of the first members to join the Society and was greatly interested in its work of honoring the memory of our Pilgrim ancestor. She was one of the contributors to the pulpit placed by the Howland Descendants in the Pilgrim Church at Plymouth and to the Howland House Fund. Her death is a great loss to the Society and the sympathy of all goes out to her family and friends.

The following tribute is from one of Kirkwood's best known citizens, who has known Mrs. Clarke for more than forty years:

Mrs. Enos Clarke

"Mrs. Mary Annette Foote Clarke was born in the old college town of Hamilton, near Utica, N. Y., the eldest daughter of the Hon. John J. and Mary C. Foote—graduated at Hamilton Female Seminary, afterwards at Miss Willard's Seminary, Troy, N. Y. Near the close of the Civil War was married to Enos Clarke. During her residence in St. Louis, she took up her new duties with great zeal, and soon became interested in the organization, and was made General Secretary of the Freedman's Relief Society, which, cöoperating with the Western Sanitary Commission furnished aid as far as possible, to those unfortunate refugees then arriving in great numbers in St. Louis.

"In Kirkwood she entered actively into all the new home relations which happily continued through many years down to the occurrence of a distressing accident by which her eyesight was nearly destroyed and gave a shock to her sensitive nervous system from which she never recovered, though her eyesight was gradually regained. During the years they lived in St. Louis she was an active member of the Congregational Church, of which Dr. Truman Post of the last generation, famous as a preacher, scholar and lecturer, was pastor, and the warm and intimate friendship between Dr. Post's family and her own maintained after the Clarkes moved to Kirkwood, down to the death of Dr. Post. In Kirkwood she was connected with the Presbyterian church.

"She possessed the good fortune of brilliant intellectual gifts, and thorough edution, and her love of reading, furnished a solace in her long imprisonment in her room, and relieved a tedium and monotony of suffering which but for this and a remarkable christian patience could not have been endured.

"A passion for flowers was part of herself, and her extensive flower beds and parterres were conspicuous among the attractions that have for years made the Clarke home one of the most beautiful places in the vicinity of St. Louis.

"Her sincerity and gentle graces endeared her to the friends who, in her early life, formed a wide circle, and even when the affliction of her later years disabled her for society and forced her to withdraw to the privacy of her own household, she continued to interchange with these friends of happier days mementoes of affection and endearment as long as they lived. D. M. G."

A Descendent of Jabez Howland Dies in San Diego, Cal.

Maj. Carver Howland, U.S.A. (retired), a former resident of Providence, R.I. is dead in San Deigo, Cal., according to advices received by relatives. While he had been in poor health for several years, it was only a few weeks ago that his illness became acute and from that time he sank gradually.

In 1902, Maj. Howland retired from the army as the result of malarial fever contracted during the Spanish war. For the last ten years he has made his home in California, believing that the climate would be beneficial to his health.

During the time that he was in the army he served almost continuously in the Fourth Infantry, although when he was promoted to be Major he was transferred to the Twenty-ninth Infantry, with which he was serving when retired.

Maj. Howland was born in Providence, R.I., and was a son of John Andrew Howland of the well-known Rhode Island family of that name. He was born in 1850. Four sisters and one brother are now living. They are Mrs. Edward S. Aldrich, Mrs. C. H. Guild, Miss Elizabeth Howland, Mrs. George H. Gurney and Joshua L. Howland. He entered Brown University in the class of 1869 after passing through the public schools of the city, but did not graduate, leaving the college to enter the United States Military Academy at West Point, where he was appointed from Rhode Island July 1, 1872.

He graduated June 15, 1876, and was commissioned Second Lieutenant in the Fourth Infantry. In the seven years following Capt. Howland saw service in the White River and other Indian campaigns in the west. He returned to West Point in 1883 and served as instructor in modern languages until 1887. He was commissioned First Lieutenant Oct. 1, 1886, and passed the examination for captaincy. Leaving West Point again in 1887 he went to the far west, where he acted as Adjutant of his old regiment. He was afterward stationed at Fort Sheridan, Illinos, near Chicago, and at Columbus Barracks, Columbus, O. He received his commission as Captain of D Company, Fourth Infantry, Feb. 3, 1894. A few years later the degree of Master of Arts was conferred on him by Brown University

When the war with Spain was begun the Fourth Infantry was made a part of the Second Division of the Fifth Army Corps and was ordered to Tampa and later to Santiago. Capt. Howland participated in the taking of Santiago, fighting bravely in the assault on El Caney.

He went tothe camp at Montauk Point with the last of the Fifth Corps, leaving Santiago Aug. 18, 1898. He collapsed from the effects of sickness and the strain when on the way to Long Island, and for a time his life was despaired of. He spent some time in the big general hospital at Montauk Point, and on recovery returned to the service. He saw some service in the Philippines, and was commissioned Major and assigned to the Twenty-ninth Regiment of Infantry Feb. 2, 1901. He served in that regiment, and was last stationed at Bencicia Barracks, California.

Maj. Howland was a member of the Society and much interested in the preservation of the old house at Plymouth. He had an autograph letter of Jabez Howland that he had planned to have framed or placed in the old house when it was restored.

The Water Mill

"Listen to the Water Mill through the livelong day
How the clicking of the wheels wears the hours away!
Languidly the Summer wind stirs the green wood leaves
From the fields the reapers sing binding up the sheaves,
And a proverb haunts my mind, as a spell is cast,
"The Mill will never grind again with water that is past"

Take the lesson to thyself, loving heart and true
Golden years are fleeting by, youth is passing too;
Learn to make the most of life, lose no happy day
Time will never bring thee back, chances swept away,
Leave no tender word unsaid, love while life shall last
"The Mill will never grind again, with water that is past."

Work while yet the daylight shines, man of strength and will
Never does the streamlet glide useless by the mill,
Wait not till tomorrow's sun shines upon thy way
All that thou canst call thine own, lies in thy today
Power, intellect and wealth may not, cannot last
"The Mill will never grind again with water that is past."

Oh! the wasted hours of life that have drifted by
Oh! the good we might have done, lost without a sigh,
Love that once we might have saved, by a single word!
Thoughts conceived but never penned, perishing unheard,
Take the proverb to thy heart, forever hold it fast
"The Mill will never grind again, with water that is past."

Our Opportunity

The opportunity has come to all Howland Descendants to help save the historic old home in Plymouth. If the old stable which so seriously menaces the safety of the Homestead should take fire some night, our dear old house would soon be a heap of ashes.

Will you not try to interest every Howland Descendant you can reach to try to help a few of us who are working earnestly—to raise the sum that is needed to purchase the old stable and tear it down? "The Mill will never grind again with water that is passed," is only too true. The opportunity is ours today. Do not let us delay but work diligently before it is too late.

This appeal is made in confidence that every Howland Descendant who reads these lines will feel a personal interest to try to assist others to help-seek out other members of your family—mail a copy of this Magazine to every one you can reach. If you are far away from Plymouth, be sure your kind help and interest will be all the more appreciated. Any subscriptions large or small will be gratefully received and promptly acknowledged by Mrs. L. B. Titus, Treasurer, Squantum, Mass.

Lady Yeardley's Guest

A CHRISTMAS BALLAD OF 1626

By Margaret J. Preston.

'Twas a Saturday night, mid-winter,
  And the snow with its sheeted pall,
Had covered the stubbled clearings
  That girdle the rude-built Hall,
But high in the deep-mouthed chimney,
  'Mid laughter and shout and din,
The children were piling Yule-logs,
  To welcome the Christmas in.

"Ah, so! We'll be glad tomorrow,"
  The mother, half-musing, said,
As she looked at the eager workers
  And laid on a sunny head
A touch as of benediction—
  "For Heaven is just as near
The father at far Patuxent
  As if he were with us here,

"So choose ye the pine and holly,
  And shake from their boughs the snow,
We'll garland the rough-hewn rafters
  As they garlanded long ago—
Or ever Sir George went sailing
  Away o'er the wild sea-foam—
In my beautiful English Sussex,
  The happy old walls of home."

She sighed—as she paused a whisper
  Set quickly all eyes a-strain—
"See! see!"—and the boy's hand pointed—
  "There's a face at the window-pane!"
One instant a ghastly terror
  Shot sudden her features o'er;
The next, and she rose unblenching,
  And opened the fast-barred door.

"Who be ye that seek admission?
  Who cometh for food and rest?
This night is a night above others
  To shelter a straying guest."
Deep out of the snowy silence
  A guttural answer broke:
"I come from the great Three Rivers,
  I am chief of the Roanoke."

Straight in through the frightened children,
  Unshrinking the Redman strode,
And loosed on the blazing hearthstone
  From his shoulders a light-borne load;
And out of the pile of deer-skins,
  With look as serene and mild,
As if it had been his cradle,
  Stepped softly--a little child.

As he chafed at the fire his fingers,
  Close pressed to the brawny knee,
The gaze that the silent savage,
  Bent on him, was strange to see.
And then, with a voice whose yearning
  The father could scarcely stem,
He said—to the children pointing—
  "I want him to be like them!

"They weep for the boy in the wigwam;
  I bring him a moon of days,
To learn of the speaking paper--
  To hear of the wiser ways,
Of the people beyond the water—
  To break with the plough the sod—
To be kind to papoose and woman—
  To pray to the white man's God."

"I give thee my hand!" and the lady
  Pressed forward with sudden cheer;
"Thou shalt eat of my Christmas pudding,
  And partake of my Christmas cheer!"
My sweethearts, this night remember,
  All strangers are kith and kin—
This night, when the dear Lord's mother
  Could find no room at the inn!"

Next morn, from the colony belfry,
  Pealed gayly the Sunday chime,
And merrily forth the people
  Flocked, keeping the Christmas time;
And the lady, with bright-eyed children
  Behind her, their lips a-smile,
And the chief in his skins and wampum,
  Came walking the narrow aisle.

Forwith, from the congregation
  Broke fiercely a sullen cry—
"Out! out! with the crafty Redskin!
  Have at him! a spy! a spy!"
And quickly from belts leaped daggers,
  And swords from their sheaths flashed bare,
And men from their seats defiant
  Sprang ready to slay him there.

But, facing the crowd with courage
As calm as a knight of yore,
Stepped bravely the fair-browed woman
  The thrust of the steel before;
And spoke with a queenly gesture,
  Her hand on the chief's brown breast—
"Ye dare not impeach my honor!
  Ye dare not insult my guest!"

They dropped at her word their weapons,
  Half-shamed, as the lady smiled
And told them the Redman's story,
  And show them the Redman's child;
And pledged them her broad plantations,
  That never would such betray
The trust that a Christian woman
  Had shown on a Christmas Day.

Sir George Yeardley (1580-1627), *was governor of Virginia*, 1616-19-21-26-27. *The Roanoke River in Virginia is formed by the junction of the Dan and the Staunton.*